Jobs If You Like...

Building Things

Charlotte Guillain

www.raintreepublishers.co.uk
Visit our website to find out
more information about
Raintree books.

To order:
☎ Phone 0845 6044371
🖹 Fax +44 (0) 1865 312263
✉ Email myorders@raintreepublishers.co.uk

Customers from outside the UK please telephone +44 1865 312262

Raintree is an imprint of Capstone Global Library
Limited, a company incorporated in England and
Wales having its registered office at 7 Pilgrim Street,
London, EC4V 6LB – Registered company number:
6695582

Edited by Rebecca Rissman, Daniel Nunn, and
Adrian Vigliano
Designed by Steve Mead
Picture research by Mica Brancic
Originated by Capstone Global Library
Printed and bound in China by South China Printing
Company

ISBN 978 1 406 24064 1 (hardback)
16 15 14 13 12
10 9 8 7 6 5 4 3 2 1

British Library Cataloguing in Publication Data
Guillain, Charlotte.
Jobs for kids who like buildings things.
624'.023-dc22
A full catalogue record for this book is available from
the British Library.

Acknowledgements
We would like to thank the following for permission to
reproduce photographs: [select]

Cover photograph of [select] reproduced with
permission of [select].

We would like to thank [name of organization or
individual] for [pronoun] invaluable help in the
preparation of this book.

Every effort has been made to contact copyright
holders of material reproduced in this book. Any
omissions will be rectified in subsequent printings if
notice is given to the publisher.

Contents

Some words are shown in bold, **like this**. You can find out what they mean by looking in the glossary.

Why does building things matter?

Do you enjoy making models or building things? People are building things around us all the time. We need people to build our homes, schools, vehicles, parks, and many other things.

Many great toys can be used to build things.

Many people work hard to build things that look fantastic!

We need to know that the things people build are strong and safe. There are many different jobs that involve building in all sorts of ways. Read on to find out more!

Be an architect

If you were an **architect**, you would plan and **design** buildings. You might have ideas for new homes, schools, offices, or airports. You might also help to repair old buildings.

Architects make detailed plans before building starts.

Architects think about who is going to use a building and what they need. They try to make their buildings strong, safe, and beautiful. Many architects try to design buildings that save energy and look good in their surroundings.

Architects make sure buildings are built following their plans.

Be a civil engineer

If you were a civil **engineer**, you could work on new bridges, roads, tunnels, airports, and other structures. You would work with **architects**, builders, and **surveyors** on each project.

Civil engineers help plan new projects and think about how much they will cost.

Civil engineers need to make sure their plans are clear. They need to be good at organizing lots of different people. They have to make sure projects run on time and don't cost too much money.

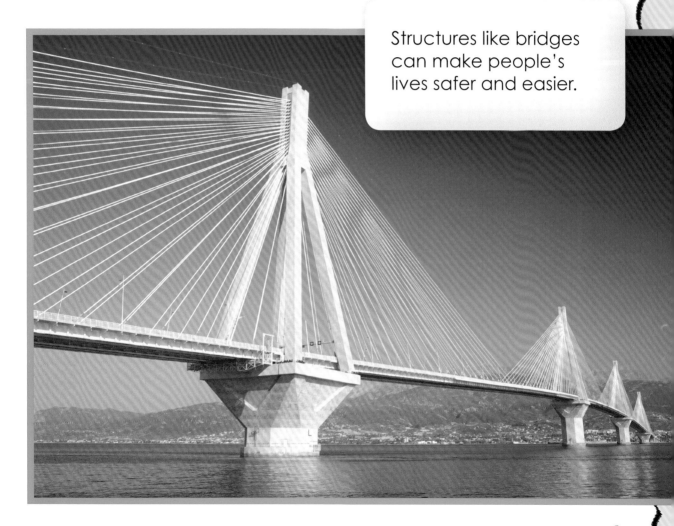

Structures like bridges can make people's lives safer and easier.

Be a landscape architect

If you were a **landscape architect**, your job would be to make open spaces look good. You might **design** the landscapes in parks, shopping centres, streets, or beside roads. You would visit the site and talk to people about what the area could look like.

Landscape architects think about many small details in their work.

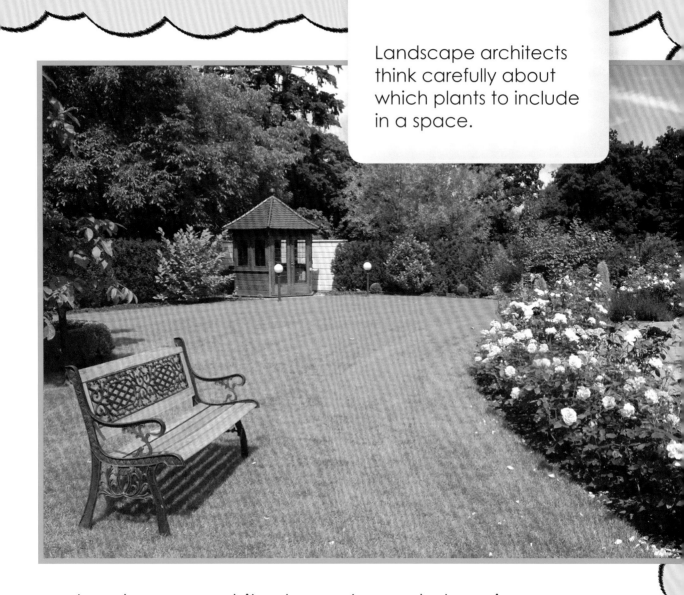

Landscape architects think carefully about which plants to include in a space.

Landscape architects want people to enjoy open spaces and care for the environment. They choose the best trees and plants for a site and think about what people need. They make sure disabled people can move around the site.

Be an electrician

Do you use a lot of electrical machines? If you do then you need an electrician to make sure everything works properly and is safe. Electricians put electrical **wiring** and **circuits** into buildings so we have all the electricity we need.

Electricians have special training to make sure they work safely.

Electricians have to check old wiring to make sure it is safe. They can also put fire alarms and other **equipment** into buildings. Some electricians make sure traffic lights work properly.

Electricians work with many interesting machines in their jobs.

Be a mechanic

Are you interested in how machines work? If so, you could be a mechanic. Mechanics check and fix vehicles and machinery, such as cars, cranes, bulldozers, and lorries.

Mechanics need to know how different machines are put together.

Mechanics check engines, tyres, and all the systems in a vehicle. Sometimes they have to take machines to pieces and repair them. Then they put the machines together again and test them to check they work properly.

Mechanics need to use a lot of tools and **equipment**.

Be a construction manager

If you were a construction manager, you would be in charge of building work. You would work with a team of builders, making sure the building follows the **architect's** plans. You would also make sure the builders work safely.

Construction managers make sure everyone is doing their job properly.

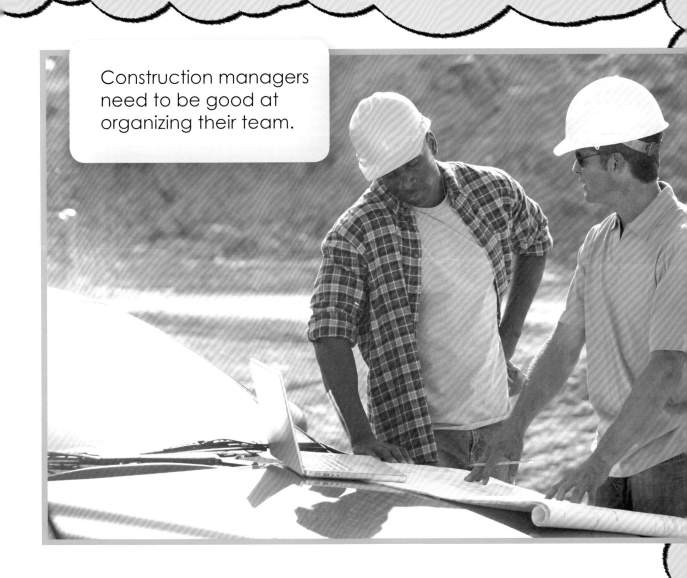

Construction managers need to be good at organizing their team.

Construction managers have to check building work is done on time. They make sure all the builders have the materials and **equipment** they need. They need to be good at talking to people and solving problems.

Be an aerospace engineer

If you love aircraft then maybe you could be an aerospace **engineer**. You might work on aeroplanes, helicopters, or even space vehicles! You could come up with new ideas for ways to build better aircraft.

Aerospace engineers need to know how different parts of an aircraft work.

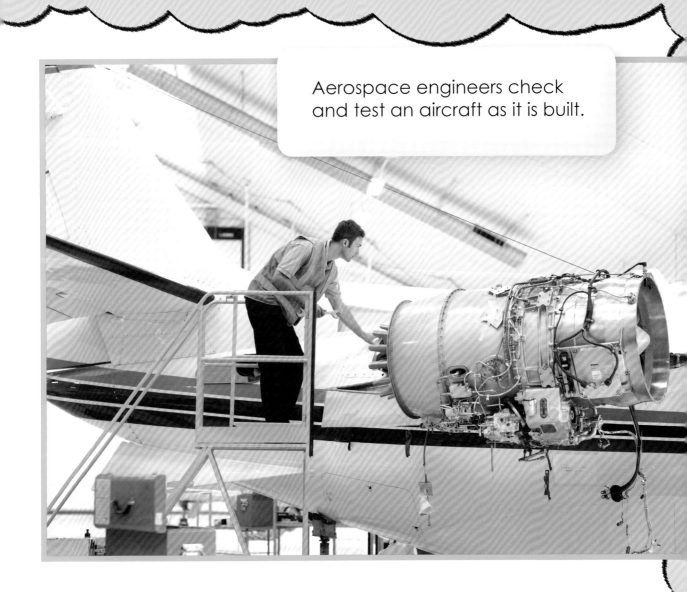

Aerospace engineers check and test an aircraft as it is built.

Aerospace engineers spend a lot of time **researching** and testing new ideas. They want new aircraft to travel fast and save energy. They use computers to **design** the plans for new aircraft. Then they check and test the vehicle as it is built.

Be a welder

If you were a welder, you would build things out of metal. You might help to make buildings or vehicles. Another part of your job could be repairing machinery made of metal.

Welders have to wear special safety gear.

Welders take pieces of metal and join them together. They have to carefully check that the pieces are joined together properly. Sometimes they cut and join plastics and other materials.

Welders have to train to do special work.

Be a set designer

If you were a set designer, your job would be to **design** the **sets** on stage in the theatre. You might also choose the backgrounds in films and television programmes. You would start by reading the **script** to get ideas on how the set should look.

Some theatre sets are moved around from place to place.

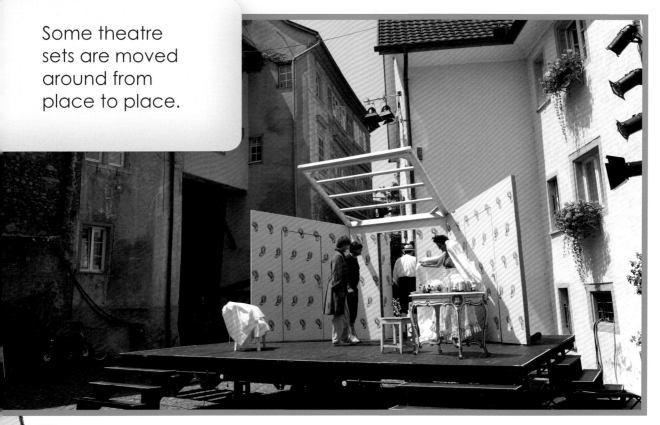

Set designers are always ready to work with new people to help tell different stories.

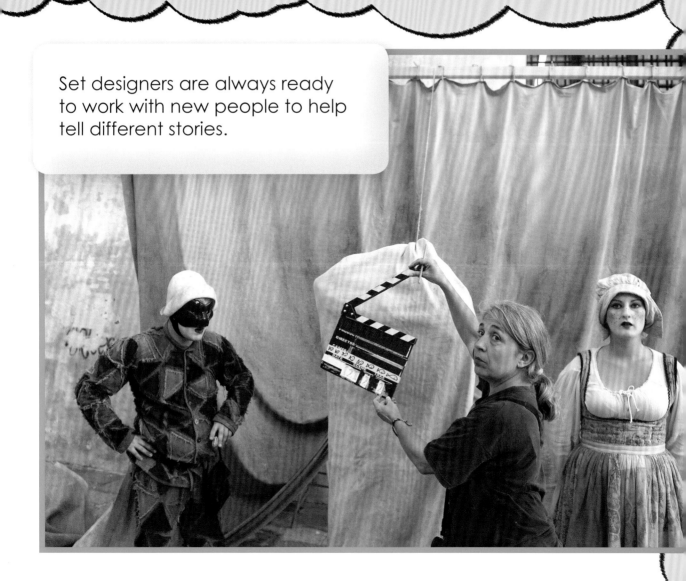

Set designers talk to the people designing costumes, lighting, and make-up. If the play or film is set in a different time or place, they find out about it. They sketch their ideas and then use a computer to design the sets.

Be a motorsport engineer

Do you love watching motor racing? Maybe you could be a motorsport **engineer**! You would **design** and develop new racing cars or motorbikes. You would spend a lot of time testing new ideas.

Motorsport engineers are always working with newer, faster technology.

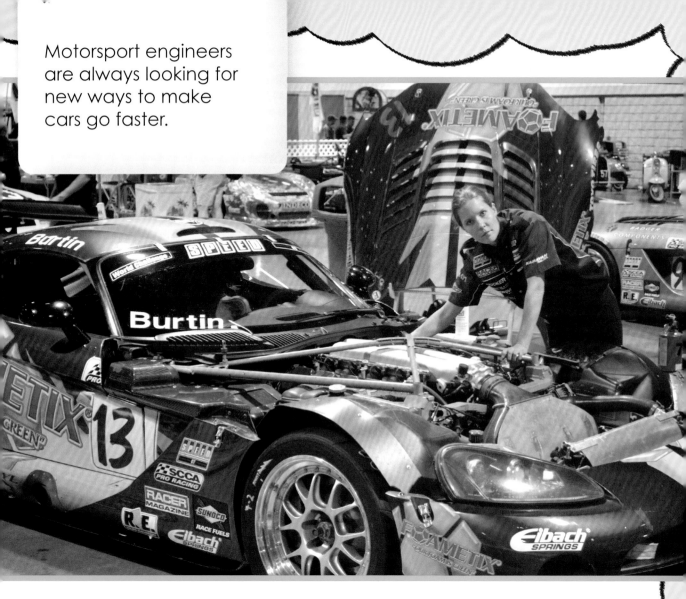

Motorsport engineers are always looking for new ways to make cars go faster.

Motorsport engineers use computers to help them design new cars. They use new materials to make their cars go faster. They keep testing the cars when they have been built to make them as fast as possible.

Choosing the right job for you

When you decide what you want to do when you grow up, don't just think about school subjects. Think about what you enjoy doing. If you are interested in plants and the environment you might like to be a **landscape architect**.

If you are mad about vehicles you might want to be an aerospace or motorsport **engineer**. There are so many different things to build, which means there is a job for everyone!

Five things you couldn't do without building things

- Live in your home
- Stand at the top of a skyscraper
- Switch on the lights or the television
- Cycle on a road
- Cross rivers on bridges

27

Building things job chart

If you want to find out more about any of the jobs in this book, start here:

	Aerospace engineer	Architect	Civil engineer	Construction manager	
You need to:	Be good at solving problems	Be good at maths and **designing**	Be good at organizing people	Be good at talking to people	
Best thing about it:	Seeing your designs in the air!	Seeing people use your buildings!	Building things that help people!	Seeing the finished building!	

Electrician	Landscape architect	Mechanic	Motorsport engineer	Set designer	Welder
Be good at following instructions	Know about plants and the environment	Know a lot about cars and machinery	Love cars	Be good at drawing	Be good at concentrating
Turning on the lights!	Making places look better!	Fixing problems!	When your car wins!	Seeing your work on the stage or screen!	You make things every day!

Glossary

architect person who designs buildings and directs how they are built

circuit path an electric current follows

design make or draw plans for something

engineer person who uses science and maths to make tools, buildings, and machines

equipment something made to be used in a special way

landscape what is around us, for example hills, woods, or skyscrapers

research find as much information about something as possible

script words that are spoken in a play, film, or television programme

set the background in a play, film, or television programme

surveyor person who studies the land or a building before construction work

wiring system of electric wires

Find out more

Polka Theatre

www.polkatheatre.com/editorial/behind-the-scenes

Visit this children's theatre website to find out more about set design.

The Landscape Institute

www.iwanttobealandscapearchitect.com/

You can watch a film on this website to see what a landscape architect does.

Index